Cow-tippi

Deep Blue Sea

Poems of Cornwall and the Atlantic Rim

Words and pictures

by Laura Harrison McBride

Muffin Dog Press

Published by
Muffin Dog Press Ltd

A CIP catalogue record for this title is available from the British Library.

ISBN-13: 978-1502717382

ISBN-10: 1502717387

Published by Muffin Dog Press, Ltd,

A Few Words About This Book and How It Came to Be

It would be easy enough to say that this book arose out of my move from the United States to the United Kingdom. It would be equally easy to say it had been percolating since my university days, since I studied the making of poems with the late Milton Kessler, himself a student, in his youth, of Theodore Roethke.

Possibly both explanations are correct, although I have often written poetry–in spurts, the way one decides for a while that the only drink worth drinking is a cosmopolitan, but then returns to gin and tonic. Just so, I have gone back and forth between poetry and lyrical writing, and journalism, and have alternately decided one or the other is the only appropriate avenue for a life's work.

All those decisions, back and forth and back again, seem now to be the hard-edged concepts of youth, something I now lack in abundance. Youth, that is. Decisions? Those I still have. But the edges have worn thin. There are places at which one decision seems to slide under or even into another, and nothing is nearly as clear as it was 40 years ago, even 20 years ago.

In short, I'm not as certain now of anything as I was years ago. Except for one thing: I have the best husband in the world. That is all. He is my dear beloved, and I expect nothing less than to be in his heart, and he in mine, for eternity.

Contents

Part I

Cornwall

Cornish spring, long awaited

Trundling down winter-scarred roads, looking
for signs. Signs that spring's balm would drift in
off the Atlantic and fill my soul again with a
Renoir of green leaves, pinkyellowblue flowers and
verdigris brooks drenching all in liquors from
the subterranean storehouse, rolling over rocks
with spitting glee and fading again into a deep, dark,
ancient peace.

I wait, craving a glimpse of the thousand shades
of young leaves. Lime. Hunter. Mustard. Forest.
Silver. Pink of copper beeches making fun of drab
neighbors with clouds of softness, welcoming.

But spring was late this year. Trees shivering, poking
out just bits of color--shy greens, dull silver,
dusty pink--and
drawing back again. Leaves huddled
against branches, clinging. Stingy,
they looked, the trees
this halting spring. Afraid
of the return of winter, afraid of a
Narnia existence, before salvation. They were
nervous, into themselves, holding back their
sumptuous spread meant for balmy air.
But it is here. Today, a Dutch blue sky holds

Cornish spring, long awaited (continued)

Floridian Gulfstream clouds floating
over Dartmoor, six miles from my door.
Clouds, sea-whipped forward across gray water off
Greenland, over Ireland to warm a bit,
and so to Cornwall. They are welcome.
A day--more?--lacking swirling mists sucking life
and hope from tree and man alike or weeks too long.

Dartmoor slumbers still, still tan, undraped with
deep green gorse's yellow blossoms. Late. Very late.
Poor lambs, mothers sheared anyway
because it is time. Winterthin ravens
hopping across the car parks,
hoping for tourist leavings but warm.
Finally.

My garden, weedy and thin, failing
like the trees to believe, yet, in spring.
Maybe today, maybe, the early roses will loosen
their buds, let their jagged leaves
relax and point gratefully earthward. Or a
shoot of muguet will poke from the compost
in the planter near the door.
My cat suns on the deck. My dog snoozes near
an open window, snuffling the mild Cornish breeze
from time to time.

I? I lurk indoors, awaiting another excuse--
to see if the tree snail noticed yesterday
is still there, to pick a flower for our Brigid
statue, to bring the May in earnest--
to wash my naked arms and face in the air I've
impatiently awaited since Samhain.

And so this is Christmas

I
Sunday, the gods of rain and wind had
their annual party. Slashing sideways
past our french doors, rain drenched the
still-green olive tree potted near the
warmth of the house. It survived last winter
and it will live through
this one, probably, if there's not
too much cold. The fields
are still green, usual in Cornwall
with its temperature-gentling Gulf
Stream passing nigh.

II
Monday it rained.

III
Tuesday it didn't rain much.

IV
Wednesday it rained and rained and rained
and rained and rained, washing the just-filled
potholes of their mix of tar and stones, water
hiding most of the axle-breakers under a front-wheel
cascade fit to soak the spark plugs. Leave the
car running while doing errands, the only way
to ensure RAC would not be called.

And so this is Christmas (continued)

V

This morning, there was a rime of frost on the
car. But the sky was bright. We drove to Tavistock
before noon, to beat the shopping crowds, to
buy a few small gifts. The Tamar had
burst its banks overnight, flooding the land
next to it on the Devon side; Cornwall's banks
are higher. The road workers had made permanent
the moveable ICE sign at a low curve in the road,
but it was just water. The fix they had done last week
had failed. The farms rose away
from the swollen brook, littered
with sheep escaping hoof-sucking lowland. Their
field was separated from fields of cows by
greybrown puffs of hedgerow trees, the
leafless branches waiting for sun to green
again. A pink rose still bloomed in the rock-made
dell before a roadside farmhouse. Every
year, heedless of rain, wind, gloom or temperature,
the rose blooms, warmed by the stone
house behind, protected by ancient walls of stone
close in all around. A walled garden
unplanned, just there, for centuries.

VI
By the time I got my coffee brewed,
the small gifts sorted
for later wrapping,
the rains had come. They pelt my
studio windows now. I don't care.
I have coffee, mince pie, a
snug home, a dog, a cat,
a husband I waited for all my
life.

VII
So this is Christmas.

Alone with rocks and seaspray

I
A friend, today, showed me a photo of
a Florida beach. Clearwater. Probably not now, not
after BP. Still, an expanse of
pristine sand, groomed before the bathers arrive, all
the umbrellas in a straight line, all the
palm trees in a straight line, awaiting
hordes of untidy people to wreck its stretched
canvas of created post-modern natural beauty.

II
Raucous. People finding toe room between
blankets tightly packed, smoking, blaring radios and
the honking nattering of women wearing too
much perfume for their age (any age) and too little
clothing.

III
Cornish beaches, full of hidey holes for the
uncommunicative finding solace
in sea scents. Rock pools, clusters of
shells, the odd bit of beach glass, less now.
Why demand plastic bottles on
the beach? I thought. Birds eat the eternal stuff
and die; Birds don't
eat glass, not when it's still a bottle, not when

Alone with rocks and seaspray (continued)

it has been wave broke, well on its way to
becoming a bit of art, or a talisman in
a pocket. Nothing tidy
about a Cornish beach. Nothing noisy,
nothing in straight, boring lines
like a computer-generated idea of paradise.

IV
Paradise.

Beach town in an old, cold country

I
Like mushrooms after a rain, they were,
wearing sunhats. Wearing shorts, sandals,
sleeveless shirts. Like people deprived
of food they were, hungering
for the taste of sun on white, white, white, white
skin. Like people longing for sleep, they nodded
in the gentle breeze. Mainly old, they were,
this weekday, snoozing without care,
casting fading eyes toward
the glistening sea, craning scrawny necks after
cormorants passing, or seagulls fighting for food.

II
The Cornish Riviera, sly token of a phrase, making
no one, no one *ever*, think of the rare atmosphere of
Cannes. Nor even Marseilles with its dark side
sloshing hard against
the swell people from St. Tropez nor even
Nice. The beautiful people have
never turned up on Cornish shores. But still,
white-skinned locals flock to Looe,
West Looe, where the beach is a rocky
strand, covered with rank seaweed, offering
up millionsmillionsmillions
of tiny bright shells, orange, maroon,

Beach town in an old, cold country (continued)

swirly purple. Offering from the sea gods to
a hundred adults no longer ashamed that
their fat upper arms squelch against the long
beach dress top, that their ankles are thick
above the flimsy sandals, and the fetching
hat fetches no stares from hunky men, but
keeps the sun off thin-skinned noses. No matter
to them. None to the sea gods.

III
There is sun. They love it. LOVE IT. Sun is
rare on the Cornish Riviera. Much
to be sought, used instantly, savored, rolled
under layers of oilskin until the next
balmy day.
Seagulls cry. And no one else. The sea air, the
warm sun, the gentle breeze
are welcome. Thanks, they say,
the old ones. Thanks. My aches
and pains were worth one more day
for this.

On my road

The old man burns wood to keep warm; a cold
spring.
Down to the nasty bits now, the wood
that disappears twixt bed and breakfast into acrid
fumes
settling in the valley.
An ancient cottage. Chimney sweep needed. No
money.
Warmth, though. But smoke seeping into
houses all round...nights, windows open, then shut
bang. Stupid old....
No, dear old soul
looking for warmth.
Bring him some soup, a pie. Embrace the old man's
fire.

The farmer, spreading cow dung. Wafting up in the
night,
wheezing of new hay growth for winter, for cows.
Stupid farmer,
making the air
a capsule of bovine germs, breathed in.

Ah.
OK then. For fat glossy cows that graze winter's
overgrowth in April, until the manure arrives.

On my road (continued)

Dear farmer, raising food, quietly, gently. Lovely
cows, calves whispering to each other in the
nights just a month past. And one bull. Not
whispering.
Laughable. Where's HIS mancave?

Lollipop lady marches on, down the lane, to the
crossing. Stick in hand
with circular STOP atop,
clad in oilskins soylent green,
flashing almost with aluminum stripes.
A cop's hat in dayglo yellow spurting
ginger hair. Wide smile, crinkly eyes, friendly
wave. Steps out, stops cars, keeps kids safe.
Marches home. Marches, she does. Getting on,
moving on.
Much to do. Farmer's wife. Good job all round.

Neighbor boys, noisy, tossing balls, jumping on a
caged trampoline.
Postie comes, dog barks, letter slot clangs. Oops.
He's back. Sign, please. Almost forgot, busy day.
Recycle's late. Tossing trash, talking trash?
Who knows? Grating gears, laboring engine,
puffing blackish smoke, environmentally sound?
Hmmm.....

Lady with big dog. Lady with small dog. Two teens,
walking and sparking (old concept, better than new).
A man and his grandson. Stop. Look at the pretty
bluebells!
Oh, no. Wet pants. Turning homeward, faster.
Cars outward, cars inward. Small van, big lorry,
motorcycles. A bike! Helmets, spandex. Giggle.
Fat. Oh well. Me, too. Sigh.

Dog's fed. Work's done. Dinner calls.
Wine, yes. Pasta and Italian chestnuts.
New home, old landscape. Good life. Good grief.
Almost missed it.
Thankful.

Enchantment enough

Dark clouds from the northwest, laden, pinned to
the earth beneath the white ones from the southwest.
Stalled, they scour'd
the land with branches torqued,
torn from trunks. They raked
the fields with hedges' trees bending low.
Like a dingy skirting board, sheep huddled
close to the base of hedgerows,
out of the rain where even bending branches
couldn't reach. Out of the north wind,
miserable despite their wool and cleverness.

A herd of black and white cows in the field
below made a photo corner, filling the triangle
made by two intersecting rows of trees
separating them from the sheep.
Fairy Cross Farm, the signboard said, intimating
enchantment, such as one might find in a
month of too much rain. Enchantment enough
to be glad one isn't a sheep.

Communication

Plymouth Sound, shining
like the pale copper edge of a new one pound coin,
wedged into the fuzzy pocket of hills
that carries the Tamar, drizzling
like icing melting on a cake
into the sea.

The mists claim the heights, here at
the edge of Dartmoor, the last vestiges
of the uplands, tied up in the knot
of gorse and ponies called Kit Hill. They
cover the roads, the mists. Ponies are fenced
here, at the bottom end of Dartmoor.

Or is it really a moor on its own? Independent.
Standing like a volcano's peak above the
suburbs of Plymouth. It's not Bodmin's.
Bodmin's too far away, seen, just, from Kit Hill
summit.

A moorish place, but softer. Here, the roads
run true from town to town. On Dartmoor,
they ramble, skirting old homesteads. Very old
homesteads, homesteads
from the Iron Age. And tors.

Kit Hill might be a tor, but it's not. Not really.

Communication (continued)

It's hollow, scraped away
from underneath by mine workings.
Barbed wire
runs around the openings,
grown over, keeping ponies
kids adults cows sheep dogs away.
No mining now,
nothing of import
to send on slender, shallow boats
down the wide brown
Tamar to its mingling
with ocean waters
in Plymouth Sound.

Kit Hill has no giant's hand construction of
rocks at its summit. Something it has, to be sure;
a man-made obelisk adorned
with disks to catch the phrases of man, slung
into phones, cast by a button push into the
universal soup. This, now,
is the communication of man, as once
a bonfire on Kit Hill, or later a message by
boat to Plymouth, to places farther on
than that. That was then, and this is now.

Far away

Saturday, seawater shattering against the ocean's
rocks,
Portmellon's seawalls, casting droplets
 pale green and light amber, like antique glass
against the muted teal ocean rising
to a steamkettle sky.

Raindrops beat a gentle lullaby on the sunroof
as we watched, dozy, for
the big swell to toss bricks of water
over the seawall, to slap onto the
seaweeded roadway. We watched, in comfort,
warm and dry, sated with aromas familiar--
coffee thermos-brought and dark and
sweet and butter cookies, and sights
odd enough, even
in rural Cornwall by the sea.

Wednesday. Small rollers approaching
Widemouth Bay, knocking student
surfers about on boogie boards,
sun forcing jackets off walkers, glinting
off fur of sleek Labradors, goofing
toward the foam. Seahissed silence
broken by the yipping of
terriers puzzled by the noise,
the scent, the lack of any holes

Far away (continued)

down which to poke a quivering nose.

Sitting on remains of an old jetty, wishing
we had coffee now, watching bright teal waves
cascade into yellowish foam, slither up the beach
between rockpools mossy and slippery and
teeming with tiny crabs, anchoring baby
mussels and other
whirl-topped shells, inedible.

Tomorrow. Monsoons again.

Such is life.

Enough for today

The storm system flowed over the tors
and down from
the moor, leaving gaps beneath it for the
setting sun to peek through, to light up
the yellow leaves atop the trees, dying
before winter but giving out one last
glimmering hint that
all is right with the world, that
such intense
beauty could only presage a beauty
of another kind
entirely. A beauty of stark gray,
black and white not
far off now. But now, while birds
stayed put for yet awhile, and even
bees still buzzed in search
of nectar, and flies sought refuge
for their final
short hours...now, the electric blue of the
storm to come, the storm that, later tonight,
would dump niagaras of water into
the Tamar Valley, now,
the leaves played as if there was no tomorrow
and, in fact, tomorrow would come. It would
come regardless of how many leaves said goodbye
to the tree, no matter how many bees got caught out
before making the hive, no matter how many

Enough for today (continued)

flies were slapped in warm houses where so many
are unaware that today, at rush hour, there was a
beauty beyond compare, a beauty enough to carry
us through the last of autumn, the browning
of remaining leaves, the dulling of the vibrant
blue of summer skies. Electric blue backing the
shining dance of yellow leaves
against the trees' still inner green. Skimming
alone below them,
a view of the alley of rounded,
glowing, shimmering
trees, watching the car's long shadow
picking out the
white lines broken down a length
of blue-gray road...
It was enough for today. Enough to carry us into a
tomorrow that would, that couldn't help but,
be just as soul-healing in its own way.

Cow-tipping and the deep blue sea

I
Cows in a broken line on the ridge, forming a
serrated edge between green field and bright
blue sky. Cloudless. Still.

II
Our car whooshed along the winding road, up and
away from the blessed beach, the acres of
grayish sand and flat stones welcoming the gentle
Atlantic swell this end-of-summer bonus day. I
didn't want to leave. The tumble of waves tossing
earth's most natural sound to my life-stressed ears
was a balm. More than the cows in their line.

III
If I tipped one cow at the top, they would roll
like spiky marbles
down the hill, across the road behind us. Maybe
they'd crash
into shoreline houses. Maybe
they'd roll down a driveway, over the cliff edge, and
into the sea.

Cow-tipping and the deep blue sea (continued)

IV
Can one ever have too much sea? Not when it is gentle, blue,
calm and approaching politely from wherever it left sometime
earlier. Not when it has receded, smooth as glass, barely lapping
the extended shelf of clean sand at low tide. Not when it is
banging its disgusted head against the cliffs, rioting after a windblown
trip across broad expanses where nothing and no one greets it for weeks on end.

V
Not ever. No, not ever. There is not a time on earth that the sea
is unwelcome.

VI
Cows give milk, and a glimpse into how we live.
The sea gives everything, and offers all the answers.

Limpets

The little town clings to the hills rising from
the small harbour, the working harbour,
a harbour that spawns fishermen. And
Fisherman's Friends. But this is
not about the untimely death
of a singer. Not a lament for the man who
lamented The Last Leviathan
and made me cry. Every time. Every time
I heard his poet's voice.

It is about life on the windy coast of Cornwall. It is
about the landscape. It is
about the messy farm atop the hill. The farm where
black earth, inked with generations of bovine
excretions, maybe blood,
perhaps petrol spills,
slithers between rock buildings and
aluminium buildings and wooden
buildings. But the house, higher up, sheltered
from the sweet sickly smell of a dairy farm.
The house, large, not too old, but still
looking as if it never gets any warmer
than yesterday's tea. Held up, like drooping
teats with an underwire bra, by iron crosses
hammered into the wall, two of them, to hold
crossbeams in place, floor
above floor. Sooner

Limpets (continued)

or later
it will tumble down.

In town, streets barely a car wide, snake
around ancient dwellings. Cornishmen
and women lived in them, do still in
some. Others cater to the ice-cream-flavoured
tastes of emmits. Emmits, Cornish for ants,
crawling from Up Country to the unspoiled shore,
spoiled
with demands for fast food, entertainment,
surfing lessons, gewgaws and
gimcracks to take back.

Above the town, a clearing offers a coast
view of big rocks, small birds.
People pulled along by dogs in coats
sniffing posts, ignoring early
daffodils seeking warmth in weak sun. Suddenly
hungry, I hare off toward Polzeath and
a beachside cafe open all year.
But cold.
"Larry, turn up the heat," the woman squawks to
a man taking not much money
in for surf lessons in his cafe back booth.
The latte was excellent.

Coastal Cornwall. Real, still, I think. Despite
emmits. Despite foreigners
like me. Some claim, I have,
to be here, having grown up on a cold island
in the north Atlantic. A sand island, not rock,
stretching out from sparkling Manhattan toward
England. Offering sea spray and even,
in my youth, a few fishermen. A few daffodils
poking out early. Horses. Chickens. Ducks. My yes,
Long Island ducks. And fresh seafood.

Like a limpet I am, clinging to anything
I can reach at the edges continents, the edges
of the sea. A fisherman's friend,
the limpet. Something to gather when fish
don't run. Limpets
are always there.
At the edge of the sea. Doing sea things.
At home by the sea.

An average Saturday

I
The sun came out. Really. It did. After
nine...maybe more...days of rain. It shone
like it had to make up for lost time. So

naturally

we took the dog to a favorite beach,
the beach with lots of rockpools at low tide--it was
low tide--that she swims in. But...the days and days
and days of storms had left mountains of smelly
seaweed between us and the pools. So
we went up to the clifftop, found a bench,
bought coffee from the kiosk and watched
as, delightfully, sailboats glided into view and

not so delightfully

Skidoos--or whatever they are called--chased
each other from up the coast to Looe Island. Even
across the water, their sound blighted the day.
But not too much.
The sun was out.

II
A lady pushed an old man in a light wheelchair to
the top of the ramp to the beach. Oh, she said,

An average Saturday (continued)

I don't know how I'm going to get you back up. But
she braced against the tarmac, holding the chair with
the sort of rounded old man in it, and got him to
the lower walkway, cement, ten feet above the high
tide and
reaching from Hannafore to West Looe. Shortly,
she came back up. No, she could not manage. I was
about to send Simon to help when the man stood,
grabbed the railing, and pulled himself along
to the top, the woman pushing the chair, encouraging
the man, whose back was a big C and whose chin,
the whole way, lolled on his chest. Poor dear.

III
A group of seashore trekkers spoke of their next
excursion,
and about leaning to scuba dive. Their dogs chased
balls.
One man left his baseball cap on the kerb. We
perched it
on the back of our bench. Soon, he returned, and was
glad to have his hat back.

IV
The wheelchair-pushing woman returned,
pushing another man, much younger
but much more frail, with twisted legs.
No walking back up for him, but,
he was lighter, and she managed.

"I'll have some muscles
after this," she said. She was a carer, not
as I first thought, a family member
of the first man. The UK does a lot better
for the disabled than the US, I thought.

V
The sun,
hot this October day,
sent us in search of
a breezy drive. Dog watered, given treats.
Off we went.

An average Saturday (continued)

VI
Another clifftop, high above surfers
at Downderry. We had salmon
sandwiches at a shaded table, listened
to the surf, watched as a few people caught
a ride on a wave, got dumped, paddled out,
did it again.
Unruly children played nearby. Why, I
wondered, would a mother let her toddler
munch Pringles all day, force-feed him a yoghurt
drink, and refuse him an ice cream with his friends?

People are strange.
The sun was out. All day.

VII
The United States is on the brink of...of what? The
lunatics, this October, have taken control of that
asylum and it's anyone's guess whether a reasonable
black man can rein in the reign of terror the Ku Klux
Teabagger
Klan has wrought. The world is frightened. But

in Cornwall

the sun was out all day.

VIII

An American dog, now called Joseph, was chained to
a tree
for four years,
hardly fed,
full of worms and bites and the saddest
face on an Alsatian I've ever seen. But
he has been saved,
his owner charged. His owner said,
"After all, he isn't human."
Did I mention the fascists in the
US Congress, this October,
wreaking misery for millions? Might as well
chain them all
to trees; they are not human. Ask
the teabaggers. Ask
John Boehner. May he live in the
infamy he has created.
But in Cornwall

the sun was out, and very hot

all day.

An average Saturday (continued)

IX
The sun was full out today. No clouds.
Well, hardly any.
Our dog played. Two disabled men
saw, smelled and heard
the blessed sea, and a lovely woman carer
risked pain to get them there. Yes,
she was paid. But not everyone
can do that job. Bless her.

X
Many old folks came out today, leaning on canes,
leaning on each other, taking in the sun, the sea,
the life-giving pleasures at the edge
of an island nation. An island nation
without steel bands or coconuts. An
island nation
mainly gloomy
in its position as a lost
part of the North Atlantic.
But not today. Today
the sun was out
all day. And
Joseph the dog, in America,
was saved.
Broken old men saw the ocean
and a lady gave

her strength to get it done. People walked,
swam, surfed, ate, gazed at the sea,
recovered from
whatever cares they carried this week.

XI
America is still stuck with
the teabaggers and
a politician whose legacy will be the like of
Hitler's, a densely packed
lexicon of how not to be human
or humane,
of how to suck the goodness
out of anything
he touches, how to send innocent people
into tailspins of despair because....
Well, because he can, and that...
that alone...

makes him the most foul creature in America.
Bar none.

XII
In Cornwall, the sun was out all day.

All day.

An average Saturday (continued)

Trees I know

I
I don't know my trees. I don't know
A sycamore from an oak, a maple
From a larch. I don't even know, really,
If England has maple trees. I know
Paris has plane trees. I know;
In a warm October sixteen years ago I
was dazzled by the dappled light
coming through the thin leaf-cladding
of the huge, smooth boulevard trees.
and I had to find out what they were.

II
I know maples, though. I do. My grandmother
had one, just one, in front of her house in
New York City. But she told me stories
of her Vermont youth, going sugaring,
tapping the trees, collecting the sap,
boiling down sugar. We always had
maple syrup on our pancakes, store
bought, but not the fake stuff. Real
maple syrup. And maple sugar, too.

III
I know the trees that one can see way
across Devon's fields, standing like giants guarding
the moors beyond. Big trees, huge trunks,

gnarled branches reaching out and reaching
up, and festooned with small leaves
all in round clumps, as if tied like so many
balloons ready for a party. I know the
smaller trees lining the roadways, their ovoid
yellow-green leaves, in fall at least, shimmering
in the last of the day's sun rays, dancing in
the breeze. I know the squat, spreading trees,
suede green lichen covering the branches,
leaves gone, decorated with deep red berries,
lots of them this year. I know those trees.
Hawthorn, deadly to cut they say. Cut, they smell
like death. Dainty white flowers in the spring,
Vibrant red berries--well, not berries, hips from
the flowers in the fall. Lichen-covered, green
suede branches. Irresistible...but resisted for
its thorns and unfortunate odour. So, then,
it's the rowan, I've learned, that one might
cut to decorate for Yule.
Two trees. I know two trees. Maybe three.
I know the sycamore.

IV
There are three big sycamores behind
my house. I don't like them. They keep the
sun out. But it is illegal to cut them down,
or at least, I would be assessed a fine. England

is serious about its green space. So am I, although
I could get a bit NIMBY about those big ugly
trees. Still, they harbour birds, and I like
birds. I feed them. I watch them. Our
cat watches them. Watches, not catches. He's
a good cat. He ate birds in his youth. Excusable.
Now, a good loud meow brings the tuna, and
That's all he wants.

V
All I want is to be surrounded by the
nameless trees, the gnarled giants,
the sparkly trees on the highway near
my home and I don't care if I know their
names. But now, as the winter
solstice approaches, I want to know one
tree, one only, for I covet the red berries on
the rowan. One rowan in my garden.
That's all I want. It's
Enough.

Old woman, hilltop, dog

I
Dodging photos all week (a peculiarity of mine, now...
now that youth is gone, pounds have arrived, hair
has turned a colour it never was), making
grocery runs, making dinner, breakfast,
sandwiches, squeezed into a car with
visitors from the States on their first
tour of England...parts anyway. Small parts,
parts I know well. Devon, Cornwall. The
coast, my first love, and
probably my deepest. Deeper even than
my love of horses, I suspect. Or maybe equal. I'm
Irish. What else? So...

II
We drove and drove last week. We drove up hills,
round
bends, through fords, weaving through the
green mazes of Cornish roads to see an offshore
island,
a Tudor house, megalithic Dartmoor, shops
in Fowey....tired, getting tired just thinking....and
other things. Magic things. Houses hugging roads,
roads
hugging forests, forests hugging hillsides. Me,
hugging myself to sleep nights. Tired. Worn out
with the demands of being a host. Happy to do it.

Old woman, hilltop, dog (continued)

Wanting a bit of the real, not the all-for-show
of National Trust or even Seaton beach,
disappointing
to my friends, Florida swimmers. Cold, gray
even in the unaccustomed
sunshine. Rocky. Odd, the river cutting
across the plage....
Oh, well. You can't win them all.
But my dog had fun.

III
Wanting, by week's end, a small reminder of
why I live here. A hint, a refresher course
of some small kind--some small moment--
that would bring to consciousness
all the eternal wonder of the place.
And then, there she was.
Tottering across the flat place at the top of
Kit Hill. So slowly, so
haltingly, held up by her stick,
holding onto a small dog
almost as tottery as she. A pair,
they were. A perfect British pair, she in her
cardigan and fluffy white hair, modest
skirt, sensible shoes. And dog, the colour of
Her Majesty's own. Around they went,
carefully, a motion picture of

Britain against a green backdrop of
present grass, faraway farmers' fields,
hedged for eons, holding goodness in their
dirt, holding permanence, holding the
wisp of an old woman and
her aged dog safe and secure
on the heights of Cornwall, as they had
always been, as they would always be.

IV
We drove home and I made dinner. We talked.
It was their last night, and my friend said
she would send the old-woman photo soon,
and she did.

Green and grey

I drove over the crest of the hill. A bright green
field stretched gently up the next rise, hedged in by
rows of brown granite rock, sliced and stood
side by side. Hawthorne, campion's pink
heads and ivy softened them. Beyond, woods ring the
town, rising green and lime and burgundy and
chartreuse, and over those,
over all of those,
the 14th century tower of the great gray church
rose to its four-spired height. St. Mellion. One
main street, one main pub,
hugging the roadway
close, twisting and dipping until
on the other side
one emerges into lowering cloud
dipping to earth
around the foot of Dartmoor. It had
rolled early across the River Tamar, hiding
Gunnislake, St. Ann's Chapel, and the sloping
quaint towns of Villaton and Pillaton, the holy
well-home of Botus Fleming, now dry, and
unnamed lands once belonging
maybe
to Cotehele, the great home started in 1300,
made Tudor later, lived in through the Great War,
surrounded now by mists

of time and place. A miracle
that any dwelling should live so long
unmolested.

The soft landscape protected it, the river bore away its
toxins,
one way or another,
for centuries.

Quiet settles over the car as it rends the mists, dodges
others rending mists. Time to step on it, time
to accelerate back to now, to home, to mundane
tasks of cooking, laundry. But
perhaps the better for having noticed the
ancient on this day, as it wrapped me in its
forever welcoming embrace
in Cornwall.

Tamar, home

I
A grey cloud, low-slung, the land's cape this morning
sitting lightly on the shoulders of Dartmoor.
Removed, now,
thin sun peeking down the valley between two moor's
hills.

A modern painting. Free and easy. Greens, verdigris,
canary yellow of rape fields shining
in the distance and framed
foreground, with the two sycamores that
define home, the birds' nesty hedgerows,
the old stones falling, leached by
filaments of plants reaching down around.

Hawthorne, gentle white flowers hiding deadly spines.
Wild campion, Pepto pink flowers on hairy stems.
Withering headless jonquil stalks. Bare paths from
badgers clumbering over, burrowing in, helping
to loose the stones. And
up again gazing toward the far distance,
not so far. Six miles only, across the Tamar
river and valley, to ancient sites. Hut circles,
ancient proof of man living,
rough-hewn, between, scallops of color.

Tamar, home (continued)

II
Vibrant, glowing in the evening sky. Hinting at
sun tomorrow, baring blue behind grey
like wool batting, floating hither, breathing puffs of
white.
Trees close in, gathered in...small woods,
remaining after centuries
Of depredations to make small houses
on a small island. Pillows, pillows of trees
softening landforms harrowed in search
of sustenance for man. Cows. Sheep. Forms
on land, lowing, cows, or sheeps' rough coughy
bark in the wilderness so close to home.
Close to dinner, enclosure from fox, badger,
man, moon, winds, rain. Moving slowly,
a stereopticon of their own making in a
landscape made by time.

A fish, I am, swimming in a slightly different,
almost parallel stream. One that holds wonders, but
only if one stops cookingthinkingwashingwritingdoing
long enough to be here
with it all. Now.

III
Forever? Who knows?
Not I.

Portmellon Storm

Seawater shattering against
the rocky seawalls, casting
droplets pale green and light
amber, like antique glass,
against the muted teal backdrop
rising to a colourless sky.
And the raindrops beat
out a lullaby on
the sunroof.

Where do fish go on
days such as this? Deep
down, into the everlasting
depths off the Cornish
coast.

We watch, comfortable in
our cars.

Part II

A Sense of Place

A Canterbury tale

I
On a Saturday, in Canterbury, I made the pilgrimage
to Becket's murder stone, the place where the
sword broke. My own Canterbury tale, long in
the making, and well appreciated. So, having a
couple of life challenges of my own (although
far short of martyrdom), I went out, behind
the cathedral, to a garden in what once were
cloisters. There
I took off my shoes.

II
I stood on the hallowed earth, sanctified with
the blood of martyrs to Henry II's juvenile
rages. A place of quantum evil, and quantum
good. Good prevails. The cathedral prevails.
The pilgrimages, whether out of curiosity, love
of art, love of religion, love of Becket, love of
Chaucer...whatever reason...the pilgrimages
to that place sanctify it, a vortex of ascendant
belief of some sort or another. For me, the
quantum, the ineffable is-ness bestowed by
centuries of longing, reaching, rejoicing, finding,
healing, is the goal.

A Canterbury tale (continued)

III
I must go back. Two hours is not enough. I barely
saw anything. I don't know that place,
not like I know St. Thomas, NYC, neo-Gothic
cathedral and my spiritual home for decades.
I didn't believe, not really, not most of the time,
in the myth. Sometimes I made a grab for it,
but it eluded me. Then I found metaphysics and
the myth became allegory, as it had always been,
though few know it. The body and blood of Christ?
Well, sure. In so far as we are all of the same
substance, now and always, and the same
quickening, now and always, mentally and
physically. But I don't care much for the
gory parts. So I've left, time and again. But
under it, oh yes, under it, I believe in the
great Word at the center of all. Not in
any one facet; all of It.

IV
And so, on the heels of my visit to that
sacred place, the hallowed ground whereon
one Henry killed a man and made him a
saint and another Henry killed a church and
gave it life, I found Life again, in metaphysics. I
took out the book, the one given me by my
great metaphysical teacher and friend, now

late. And I opened it, ran my hand over the
inscription in purple ink, felt the wisdom
of my beloved friend, my mentor course
into me. I could feel him sitting there, in my
late summer greenhouse with me, fending
off the chill early north wind with coffee, buckets
and buckets of coffee. And his twinkly eyes,
rolling in mock horror at something crass I'd
said. Or looking gently at me, loving me
as no other friend ever has.

V
Well, that's that, then. My beloved mentor has
returned
to me, returned me to the quantum fields in
which everything lives and has its being, quick or
dead, once and forever.

VI
My pilgrimage continues, but with a lighter
heart.

A Canterbury tale (continued)

I've flown away

I
A memory washed over me this morning, as
I washed dishes. I felt just as if I were sitting in
a rather annoying airport food court. Well, not
really a food court. Just a bunch of ugly tables and
uncomfortable chairs. It was bright, too bright,
the big windows supplemented by fluorescent
lights hanging down on stalks from the hangar-
like ceiling. Blue, dark blue, I think was the colour
of the pleather on the chairs. What did we eat?
I don't know.
Why were we here?
I don't know. It wasn't our
usual airport. It wasn't JFK in NY.
It might have been
LaGuardia. Maybe.
Rarely flew from there. Not
Newark...because there is a god (just a turn of
phrase signifying nothing) and so we could
avoid that one.

II
Anyway, I used to spend quite a bit of time
in airport travel lounges and restaurants. Not
for years, though. I guess I liked it, for a while.
The frisson of knowing I was getting on something
that is impossible, can't possibly work, to go

someplace I wanted to go. Those days,
before the NSA poisoned
adventure, it was only mildly annoying and
the payoff was worth it. Not now. No, not
since we moved to the UK so we could see
the EU without flying. Boat, train, car on train, car on
boat. No airports. But we haven't
done it yet. Three flights, Cyprus and
Malta (too long and hard to drive and ferry,
but it COULD be done) and
Italy. Quick trip, too far to drive in
the time.

III
It has been two years since the Malta trip. None
since, not farther than Suffolk. Oh, sure, we said
we wanted to go to the Scilly Isles. Or the Isle of
Man. Jersey. Guernsey. You can take a boat. Or
Dublin; car, boat, car.
But we sit here, building a greenhouse, burying
an old dog well-loved, adopting a new dog soon
to be set gently down out of New Dog Status to
Dog in Training. Heel, come, sit, stay.
NO CHEWING.
We seem to have become old and settled, but
I am unsettled.
I am not done yet. So, despite

it all--the aches of age, the finances of post-Bush,
the satisfaction with having left decaying
America behind forever, missing
my distant horse, wondering if
I will ever see my brother again--I
seem to end up in airport lounges via quantum
synapse leaps of a brain that has seen
far too much, and possibly
not enough.

IV
We have a small trip coming up, by car. Taking
the young dog to Canterbury. She doesn't care;
I do. I love Chaucer's bawdy tales. Want to see
the cathedral. Yes, I know. Half-timbered houses
are long gone. I think maybe Canterbury is
ugly now. No matter. It's a trip. It will be good
to get away. Welcome Breaks on the motorways
are not as studiously clinical as an airport
lounge. No terrorist-hunters lurking in the
hallways to force you through the ray-tube to
find your body's secrets. Lord,
can you believe Paris airports?
It was at least six years ago when we left Paris
early, went to Orly rather than DeGaulle, and
still, combat-booted, machine-gun toting French
militaristic gendarmes (or are they police-like
soldiers?) patrolling the whole bloody thing.

I've flown away (continued)

V
We had better do it, that train-car trip to France
and Spain. We need to do it soon. I can't spend
busy mornings pining for horrid airport lounges
when I'm not dead yet. I need to make some new
memories, manufacture some new passions for
some new favourites.

VI
I think I need to fly away, but not by air. I need
to smell new smells, feel new air currents on my
skin, see new buildings. Not trees. If you've seen one,
you've seen them all. No, the works of humankind,
that's what I need. An infusion of the different, the
exotic, the not me.
Soon.

River valleys, home

I

The wind flows around the
house. Noisily. A substrate
forming thoughts and the
low thrum of the space heater
giving the central system some
help on this bleak day.

I turn my head toward the french doors,
with the young potted olive tree
swaying,
notice the ancient sycamore in
the hedgerow beyond
letting its bare branches do a
hula around its solid trunk.

Bluegrey, the sky is. The
sky over Dartmoor, distant
across the River Tamar, and
valley, deep into South Devon. A
herd of red Devon cattle, a compact
breed, good for eking out a life
on land as lean as any, but
teeming with life all the same.

II

River valleys, home (continued)

I would sit, sometimes, in
the big living room on the
sixteenth floor, gazing at the low
buildings across the street, catching
a glimpse of the Hudson down
the cross streets in my
confused section of midtown
Manhattan. The Clinton Neighborhood
began here, at Eighth Avenue. It was
once, Hell's Kitchen, but had been
gentrified, first in name, later in
fact as strivers replaced the
previous population of immigrants
from Ireland first, Puerto Rico later.

The theater district begins behind
my building, at the Alvin Theatre.
Broadway slices through
the cement island a long
block behind my building. My
building. As if I owned it, not simply
leased use of one of its
347 apartments. We all
say--said--that, New Yorkers.
It was my building, my super (New Yorkese

for head maintenance man), my hallway, my subway line. The A train, like the swing song. I took it often.

The lights twinkled across the river, in New Jersey. The sky closed. It did. Night didn't fall in Manhattan, as elsewhere. No. The sky closed, starting in Jersey, coming across the river, rolling back another bit as each street of tall buildings came between it and me. The sounds change when the sky closes. Taxis, strident, pushy on their daily way up Eighth Avenue, seductive now as they bring workers home to a night on the town, perhaps. Or to visit a friend, in Yorkville perhaps, on the upper East Side. The horns get more posh as they head that way.

The whirr of a bike messenger's bell as he darts through traffic, his last delivery, or homeward bound. A shout here a crying child perhaps. Sounds travel up the stone sides of buildings, you know, as if the buildings were the smooth slopes of a glaciered mountain. Doesn't matter how high you are, there's noise. Except above the setback, the place where the

building sucks itself in, perches two or
three floors of smaller, pricier apartments with
balconies so people might only fall to the
setback space below, not 20 stories to
the ground. Those who pay can live, quiet
and in no danger. It's quiet there, above the
setback. There, the noise follows
the line of the building from the street,
up and beyond the posh apartments, zooming
onward at the speed of sound into the waiting
atmosphere.

The night sky in Manhattan is
not black, not indigo. It is charcoal
grey. Shimmering right up to heaven,
wavering in its own light source like
an old bit of film noir, viewed through
frosted glass.

III
The night sky is on its way to
Cornwall now, the colour
of the blue-green ocean on a
stormy day, trolling across the
landscape, pulling great
massed clouds within its
fulsome body. Dartmoor

forms a ribbon out over
a misty middle reach, a
thousand miles from the
silhouettes of summer's toys,
draped in plastic on my deck.

The soul I brought to earth: Solstice song

How far have we wandered? In the 1970s,
the pre-eminent archaeologist in Ireland
told me that Newgrange
was no more than a pagan tomb. I
disbelieved him. I had climbed
a vertical ladder in Donegal,
down into another such souterrain
and knew
in my bones
that it was more. But growing up, no one
said anything about a solstice
except the science
teacher. We celebrated July 4
with firecrackers,
drunken adults,
watermelon pit-spitting fights among
us kids. No flowers.
No acknowledgement in that
crass holiday celebrating, now,
a republic early on
the skids, unlikely to last even
half as long as Rome.
Another story for another day.

The soul I brought to earth: Solstice song (continued)

This day sees gloom in my town, sun in a
friend's.
If there were
a Newgrange here,
no sighting of bright light
on dim underground walls would
happen.

I haven't celebrated the solstice,
and don't expect to. Unless
it was my visit to the art store,
to buy a frame
to complete a gift for a farm wife I know
who let me photograph her at her
day job, Lollipop
Lady of Drakewalls.

Maybe that's my celebration, then.
She knows the ways of the planets,
the earth, the sun, the moon and
living things. She knows the people
in the valley. She owns cows, like
a Celtic princess of old. She is
kind and wise.

Yes, that will have to do, as I emerge
from the concrete chrysalis
of birth into a modern US life
into the waning of it
among the neo-Druids of Cornwall.
I gasp for air, I turn wherever
I must to seek the sun. Finally, I can
look at the pale light reaching out
to my distressed fuchsia and
revel in the rebirth, however slow, however
halting, of the soul I brought to earth.

Slainte.

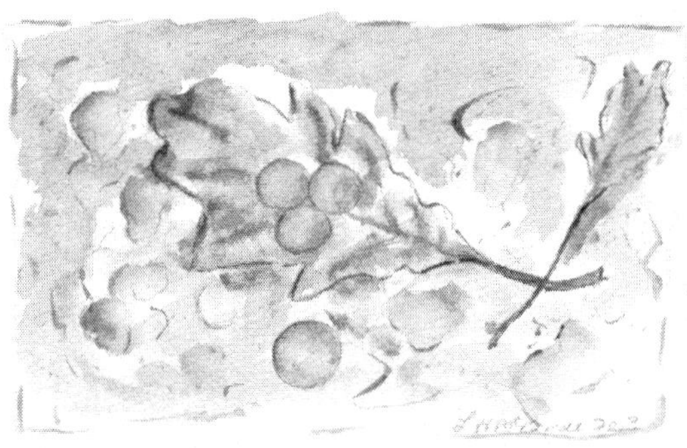

Drogheda

I

Strong, sweet, milky tea, and
a plate of biscuits. Nothing fancy.
Nothing fancy at all. Plain biscuits, perhaps
one with pink icing, hard as a rock, or
white. And digestives. Digestive biscuits
like wholemeal treats, an oxymoron.
Nothing special.
Tea in a stainless steel pot, milk in
a white jug, on the brown bakelite
tray with a white tray cloth. And sugar.
Lumps in a plain white bowl, and tongs.
The sofas were not too deep, the rug on the
lino not too old. The room warm enough. It
was up the stairs off reception, the lounge,
or TV room, or whatever you'd call it in the
pre-Euro days of the early 1980s, when
Ireland was just beginning to warm to the
swell, the fashionable, the trendy. But not
there, not at the White Horse Hotel in
Drogheda.

Drogheda (continued)

II
The second trip it was, I think, when we found
ourselves in the grey city of Drogheda, on our way
someplace. Who knows? Writing for business
magazines, going where we were sent. But
it was delicious. Having tea, brought up by a
polite, kind receptionist, on a sunny afternoon
in a grey city in a green country. It was delicious,
for Yanks, tingling with the unsavory thoughts
of Cromwell lopping heads, posting them beside
the cathedral to chasten any papists still about.
There are papists still about in Ireland, in
Drogheda, even, thank the lord, despite
British attempts to cull them
like so many unwanted badgers.
Not that I'm any fan of the Pope, but it is theirs,
the Catholic thing, supplanting the old ways,
but still.....
Anyway, the old ways linger, in the pubs where
community is all and religion less than nothing.
In shops, where Celtic hospitality transcends
the need to make a living. In restaurants, where
diners' comfort cannot be too much catered for
by managers cut from the cloth of an old civilization
dressed in new pinstripes and silken ties.

III

Those heads, shrinking on the cathedral walls.
Cromwell, slayer of the good and craven toady
to an unkind god. Burned priests and monks alive,
slew civilians as coldly as combatants. Earned his
hatred in Ireland, so he did. To this day. To
this very day.

IV

Strong, sweet, milky tea, a couple of tiny mince pies,
and it all returns to a mind that should by rights,
have forgotten a lot more by now. The sweet
calm air of the White Horse lounge. The snoozy
feeling,
so welcome after a day's drive
from one factory town to
the next, a winding down between gigs, paying
gigs that let me see the green land as often as I liked,
almost. "Have pen, will travel." A long
time ago, now, it seems. I hung up my traveling bag
and packet of pens two decades since.
But all it takes is one grey day, one cup of strong,
sweet, milky tea and it lives again. The grey cathedral
walls, not festooned with Catholic heads this lifetime
(there is no linear time, you know), but
singing to me with voices both angelic and demonic,
blending the sacred land with the round-headed
Satan from just across the Irish Sea. The warm,

silent lounge, deep within an old hotel, a hotel
whose walls might have embraced
Cromwell. Oh glory please no.

But still, once tasted, those small moments of
strong, sweet, milky tea remain, washing away
the troubling thoughts of horrors
long ago, of challenges yet ahead.
Strong, sweet, milky tea. Balm. Absolution
of a sort. For all of us,
for everything.

The History of Man in 360 Degrees

I
I touched one of the stones today, one of the
triangular stones sunk deep into the peaty
ground on Dartmoor. The entrance to a hut,
or so I'm told. A line of stones, also countersunk
into the earth, marches over
the gentle rise, toward a stream cutting through
the manicured pastures below the windswept
meadow below Cox Tor. One of the stones
had broken in the recent storms, a pink section
falling away, leaving the interior of the stone--pink
flecked with grey--revealed for the very first
time ever. We walked on.

II
You can see the whole world from there, from the
slope
below Cox Tor. Not directly, no. But you can see
to Plymouth Sound where the children
of a vicious god sailed into the cruel
north Atlantic, to seek solace. Solace
in their own cruel, unforgiving society, still
holding a land in fear, heaping ignominy on it in the
name of a god most of the globe rejects in
favour of lesser, but kinder, gods.
Here, where there are hints of the world

that was, long before your time, the gods had to be
kind, because the landscape was so harsh.
Those old gods, the kinder gods, offer
up few of their secrets to us now...but
I want to know. I need to know how it was,
in time, space and spirit, for the hutmen
who lived in stone on stone, high above
their fellow men.

III
Hut circles dot Dartmoor, broken up, the
remains covered now by layers of dirt and
botanic material. It looks like turf, my
husband said, pointing at a bit of moss-covered
sodden ground near a hut's ancient doorway.
Turf for burning for warmth, like Ireland's peat,
which comes from boggy moors.

IV
Brent Tor's pinnacle seems to waver over the
distance of cold March air. St. Michael de Rupe,
ancient church, rises like pumice breaking
earth from the tor's top. A penance, the climb to
that odd Christian implant. A demanding god
doubtless lives there, beckoning the odd pilgrim
on the odd Sunday when services' candles light
the rocky building's inner gloom. How can

spirits soar in such a place? Nearer heaven,
perhaps. But tethered to a religion of jealous
gods, murdered saints, mischief on a global
scale. Crusades, Inquisitions. Who can feel
connected to the good in a temple to such
things?

But this day, a glider spreads joy, flashes
its wings circling grey, forbidding Brent Tor, making
for the lowland on the draughts of wind
this sunny, still unsettled day.

V
Ponies gather round
in the car park where the Willy's ice cream van
waits beckoning, offering treats for kids and
greedy crows all the year. All the year, rain or
snow, warm or
cold.

VI
Whitchurch Down rises bracken brown
next to early greenfields,
growing fodder in the middle distance.
Tavistock, "Ancient Stannary Town," huddles
in the far distance. Thriving once on
the hard-won products of tin mines dotting
the moor, it now thrives on the thin wallets

The History of Man in 360 Degrees (continued)

of old people, and the fatter wallets of
day trippers seeking to add another check
mark to their bucket lists. "Seen Dartmoor, we
did," and he boards the bus satisfied in
what the world has offered his unsophisticated
old bones. "Had a Devon Cream Tea, too," he
said. "Can't say as the cream was any diff'rent
from home, and the scones warn't as good as
Sally's. Ponies were cute." Heedless of the eons
of living there, by people just like him.

VII
We can see our house, eight or nine miles away,
from the meadow below Cox Tor. A road winds
down off the moor, down Pork Hill, past the
pricey boarding schools, into Tavistock, and
out again, down and down and down through
woodlands to the River Tamar. Unseen through
thickets, the 1527 bridge of gray stone takes
us toward home, over the river swollen by
three months of rain, sleet, hail. The wettest
winter in 250 years, not long on Dartmoor.

VIII
I must complete an item on my bucket list
this summer. I must lie naked on Dartmoor. Not
on a blanket. Just me, my skin, on the soft short

grass clipped by thousands of woolly
sheep, at large, always, on the open, communal
moor. There are ticks in the grass, they say, from
the sheep, the foxes, the odd deer perhaps. Don't
do it, they say.

I've had ticks before, I say. Pick them out,
no harm done. The surface
of my skin must touch the surface
of the earth, just here, just
in this way. I have been longing
to do it, jumping, one might say, out of
my skin to do it. Put off one
summer by rain, another by cold, another by
the arrival of houseguests one
after another.
I will be put off no longer. Not by ticks. Not by rain.
Not by cold or people who wouldn't understand.
My skin must touch the skin of the earth. It must.
It will not be denied. The heaven of history, absorbed
and felt. There must be a communion sanctioned
only by the spirit in me
craving the knowledge of all that ever was, craving
the eternal that is Dartmoor.

IX

The earth of Dartmoor, trod for eons by species
large and small, showing its inner self in massive

The History of Man in 360 Degrees (continued)

outcrops, giving its life in sparkling streams, covering its naked power in a soft tissue of dark earth and bright green grasses. The air, swirling above and around, carries the very breath of the ancients. We all breathe bits of air breathed once by ancient Greeks. Or ancient hutmen on Dartmoor. There must be more essence of hutmen, one might suppose, lingering around the place they lived and loved, were born and died.

Key West Suite

I
Pan Am. What's that, then? Oh,
simple, really. It was founded in
Key West, Isle of Bones, Cayo
Hueso. The gray house was first
an art shop, a decade later a
restaurant with a white piano
bar. The Pigeon House Patio. Then
again, bigger. Not good. No. But
Pan Am is gone, too. What else?

II
The Raw Bar preceded Buffett, and
it will probably last beyond him. The
air-conditioning will go (one hopes) and
the floral-clad real housewives of Ohio and
their wimpy husbands and then, the
waitresses with dirty faces and dirty
minds can return, and the oyster
shuckers missing fingers (of course) and
the real people sitting on long benches
eating real seafood and the best Key
Lime Pie in the archipelago. When
Buffett leaves. It's not Margaritaville. Hell,
Key West is rotgut booze in chipped glassware,
or at least, it was. Before Buffett. Before the
Disney cruise ships. Before forpetessake Fendi

or some other Eurotrash retailer shoved
out Kavanagh's venerable tacky import
shop, sent Key West Fabrics out of the water
front, and sent conches and clued-in visitors
scurrying for the ass-end of the island just
to avoid modern dross and ten dollar
cups of coffee.

III
Key West. Hemingway. Pressed his last penny,
he said, into the cement of the pool his second
wife had installed. Tennessee Williams. Real talents
used to live there. Oh, sure. Buffett's a real talent.
But he should have left Key West alone, as Papa did,
and
Mr. Williams. They didn't have the wealth Jimmy has
(yes, that Buffett, not Warren). They were tortured
artists of the classic kind.

IV
I met Mr. Williams once, when he was polishing off
a lot of wine with friends on the deck at the Pier
House. Intimidating. But thrilling, in a way shopping
at the Margaritaville shop, junking up Duval where
a divey bar used to be, will never be. Unless, of course,
you are a flower-clad real housewife of Ohio.

Paradise and pelicans

I
Islands call me. They always have. First,
Long Island, where I was born in the New
York City borough of Brooklyn. And later,
Manhattan, my New York island of choice.

II
But not until I had already discovered an isle
like no other. An island closer to Cuba than
Miami. An island where the natives are as
indolent as hogs in slop, as interesting
as any band of remote inhabitants of
the earth. Conchs, they're called. Skin
tanned the color of tobacco, hair bleached
if it's not black to start, muscles taught
from all that indolence. By which I mean
catching fish...when the spirit moves them. Or
guiding tours...when the spirit moves them. Or
writing books...when the spirit moves them. Or
painting. Or opening a gin mill. As long as
the spirit moves them. Failing that? Well, there's sun
and sand and water and boats and mangoes
falling out of trees and avocados if you're lucky
and the odd shopping at Fausto's. At dusk, go
to Smather's Beach, buy a coffee, sit on a bench in
the bandshell and watch as pelicans dive for
their daily bread. Make young boys' bomber noises

as the huge beaks pierce the still lagoon-like waters,
and splutter like a cartoon cat when the pelican
comes
back up. Gulp when he does. Simple pleasures of
island life.

III
Watch the tourists turn Red From the Sun,
and be sure to tell them you are Laura From the
Earth...
or whoever you are. Or don't do it. Just laugh. Strut
on
back into town. It's not far. The whole island is two
miles by
four. Find some dinner, Italian if you're broke, island
cuisine if you're flush. Or the Raw Bar. It's OK, just,
since Jimmy Buffett bought it. No more paper plates,
though, and air-conditioning. On the shrimp piers for
goodness sake....a/c. But still. Well, OK. A shadow of
its glory days, men missing fingers, waitresses in
shocking short shorts and few teeth and stringy
hair. Rough. Smooth now, Ohio tourists in panel
shirts, cameras in expensive leather bags. But still,
it is the Raw Bar. Oysters. Clams. Shrimp. Fish.
Some
cooked. Some not. With slaw and fries.

IV
But the Key Lime Pie...well, theirs and the pie
of the old burned-down Big Pine Lodge 30 miles
up the keys. You haven't had either? Pity. Yes, pity.
Some things must be experienced. A treasure of my
life, those. Along with the view from the Pier House.

V
A trendy hotel, first in Key West as the 60s turned
from hippie heaven to yuppie hell. But still...
the best outdoor bar on the planet. See for
yourself. Bend your elbow, stay a while, drift
into the flow of talk of locals, rich visitors and
bartenders with a lot to say. Get sleepy. Shuffle
on back to the hotel you can afford. Do it again
tomorrow.

VI
Heaven.

The Center of the Universe

I had the privilege of being born in Brooklyn, NY, thus carrying on a proud family tradition, and joining the ranks of writers also born there, a list that includes Woody Allen, Ken Auletta, and Norman Mailer, as well as songwriter Carole King, poet Walt Whitman and...just for fun...iconic deejay Wolfman Jack. (I saw the Wolfman and danced to his discs at a club in Coconut Grove, Florida in the early 1980s. That had to be a seminal experience for radio-raised boomers, I always thought.)

Anyway, I spent a good deal of my life in and around New York City, and even when I was not in it, it has always formed the substrate for everything else. Everything else.

When I decided writing a poem might be a good way to flex writing muscles after a bout of the flu, I came across this watercolour. I probably painted it in about 1980. I painted a lot of New York scenes then, including one from my apartment window in Brooklyn, looking across the harbour at lower Manhattan and including the Twin Towers. I will never sell that one.

This one was looking out the window of the Opera Cafe, directly across from Lincoln Center. I was looking at the second floor lobby of Avery Fisher

Hall, and very likely drinking very strong coffee and eating one of New York's finest pastries. It might well have been that day that a young comedienne and her agent were in the booth behind me. She was trying out punchlines. (First you must know that, back then, rents could only rise with each renewal by a certain amount under the Rent Stabilization Act, now long gone, more's the pity.) She said, "I live in a rent-controlled apartment." A brief pause. "Yeah. My rent controls my life."

I've never forgotten that, anymore than I have forgotten the images of the next poem.

The Center of the Universe

I
Yes, I did spell it the American way. I had to. It is
the center of the universe, and American
in a way, but not totally. Oh, no. New York is
itself. It is the dirty, noisy, 24/7 personification
of a god of Yaaaahhhhhh. That god,
the god of Yaaahhhhhh, has decreed that
all New York cabbies should either
kibbitz with passengers, or
not be able to speak English beyond
"Hihowareya,"
which is taught to all cabbies
before they
are permitted to release
the parking break their first day.

II
The god has decreed that the smell of
chestnuts roasting
on a handcart with a fire down below,
in front of St. Patrick's Cathedral at
Christmastime
will get in your nostrils
and stay there, whether or not
you actually spring for a bag
and eat them, for the
rest of your life. And you will yearn.

III
You will yearn for the rumble of the
subway, heard through gratings on which
the homeless sleep at night, wrapped in
rags, tucked in on an old packing carton
they drag around
all day in their shopping cart. They might
spit at you. They
might not. Depends.
Like NYC depends. It is, frankly,
everything. Every blasted thing
there is in the universe bar none.
No farms, you say. Really? What about
the pocket farms on rooftops,
in the boroughs beyond Manhattan?
Large animals? HAH. Got ya.
There are riding stables in Manhattan,
Brooklyn, Queens, the Bronx and Staten Island.
So there.
OK. There are no cows, now.
But there used to be. They were kept
in Central Park and milked
for the benefit of school children.
And there were sheep in the section
of Central Park called
The Sheep Meadow. Well, duh.
Great shopping emporiums. Broadway.

More restaurants
than you could visit if you ate
every single meal out
for the rest of your life.
History. Fraunces Tavern.
Money. The Stock
Exchange. Knowledge. The
New York Public Library,
Fifth Avenue, "Please don't feed the stone lions."
Yes, you. Don't leave your rotten
candy wrappers there. Whadya think
this is, a gahbage pit?
(And don't remove the wreaths at
Christmas, either. Buy a damn
souvenir, will ya?)

IV
New York survived the Revolution,
the War of 1812, the Civil War,
both
world wars and mayors
as bad as
Michael Bloomberg. All it takes,
every so often, is one great one,
an Ed Koch for instance,
to resurrect the place,
to please the god Yaaaahhhhhh.
Meanwhile,

The Center of the Universe (continued)

New Yorkers look after it. Not
the Eurotrash international
fiduciary bounders rockstars shitheads
who seem to be in charge sometimes.
No.
New Yawkas. People with accents
stranger than fiction, and
hearts as big as Fort Knox. Closed lips,
though, until you are
in need, or show them a laugh or two. Self-possessed,
New Yorkers are.
And why not? Their rent controls their lives, but still
they enjoy. It is all about enjoy. Life. Bigger than life
life. New York, my hometown.

Ocean Avenue, Brooklyn

I
There's a certain cast of sky that always
reminds me of Ocean Avenue in
Brooklyn, New York. I didn't live on
Ocean Avenue in Brooklyn, NY. My
cousins did. Four of them, evenly divided
between girls and boys. One of the latter
was my "kissin' cousin"....
Odd term, that. They were all close
enough to be kissed. But one was my
soulmate. Is now and always shall be.

II
We lost each other for 25 years, but
found each other again, less than an hour apart.
And we loved each other, again,
as in youth. When we painted together. When
he tried to make me more religious. When I
couldn't understand what he saw in
becoming a priest. He didn't. He
got drafted instead and a Vietcong
bomb had a bit of a tussle with him which
he eventually won.

III
My cousin was the first person to tell me when I
had reached womanhood, a comment on

filling my bra. He is two years older.
I was the only person to refuse to comment,
all those separated years,
when other family snidely asked me if
he were gay. Ask him, I always said.
That means yes, right? No. It means ask him.
He is. I knew. None of them really cared
if he was or
if he wasn't. They just wanted to know. But
it was his to tell. Uncle Nicky--my father--
never knew,
not from me, before he died. My cousin
loved Uncle Nicky, missed his funeral because
he didn't know. He didn't know how anyone
but me
would feel about his being gay.

IV
Ocean Avenue, Brooklyn, New York. Big,
wide street, white, back then. Not
the pavement, the faces. Jewish and Irish, maybe
some Italians. Now
black. Jamaicans, other islanders, mainly
I think.
Still a lovely boulevard, and why not?

V
Ocean Avenue, Brooklyn, New York, where the
late sunlight of a winter's day slides in over
low-rise apartment blocks.
Filtered sunlight of early fall shifts
among the crannies in the
pre-war buildings, embellished, fronted with
tall maple trees sometimes. Lacey
tracery of leaves. A church's iron
fence and gate makes a grid. Hopscotch.
Counting shadows instead of cracks,
perhaps. Or just walking slowly,
listening to the sparrows in the churchyard's
trees. Noise abates in mind, if not
in fact. The horns of traffic
roaring by
are a silence all their own.

VI
A soft blue-gray, slanting rays of milky colour
drift across the wide avenue. Six p.m. New Yorkers
running hither and thither (a phrase they would
not use, but still) on their errands. There
are always errands. One errand, usually, was
to take my cousin's' dog for a walk. He would
tell me, on the way, stories of his days at school,
plaguing the nuns with his impertinence until
I suspect, they encouraged a vocation, to get

him gone, get him to a monastery asap. But
it didn't take. I knew
it didn't take when he told the joke about
the mother superior's diarrhea. Whew.
Close one. I didn't want him cloistered
away from me.

VII
I haven't seen him in four years now. We seldom
write, phone less. A childhood
together, an adulthood separated, a seven-year
interlude
together again. And now we are apart.
I miss him. But I have him. He is the heart of my
heart, the riotous balance to my quieter ways,
the male to my female, the eternally hopeful
to my frequent depressions.
I love my cousin. This one best of all.
He knows, I know, we all know.

VIII
Sometimes, a play of light over the cliffs at a
Cornish beach sends me back to Ocean Avenue.
To the smell of nearby elevated trains, to
the slight fear some gang of boys might come
upon me unprotected and hurt me with
cruel words, meant to make a scrawny girl cringe, to

pump them up. I go up in the rattly elevator
in my heart to
my cousin's home, where my aunt
would hold sway like an Irish queen, a
Grainne in black (dyed) sausage curls,
red lips and lounging pajamas in faux
silk.
We called her, later, La Te Da for her fancy
ways. My cousin is plainer. So am I.
We laughed. We always laughed.
We would now. We would. But years and
fears and oceans keep us where,
I suppose,
we should be. Living, remembering,
having those Pepsi-drinking, watercolour-painting,
always talking, ever loving
days of two small youths hanging out
on a very long street in a
very, very big city where nothing ever ends.
And so it is,
always was and ever shall be.

Christmas in New York

I
One year, we had no money. Well, not much
money. So I went to the library at Lincoln
Center, a performing arts library, checked out
two or three beautiful albums--vinyl, back then--
wrapped them and gave them to my
husband as a temporary Christmas gift,
along with some other little gifts. It was
OK.

II
Manhattan at Christmas is a feast that costs
nothing, as long as you have a roof over
your head and enough food money. Some years,
the lean first years, we bought clothes
at second-hand shops. But in Manhattan, you
get Brooks Brothers suits for ten bucks. Take
such suits to a tailor, for ten more it will
look handmade for you. You can wear that
swell suit to churches where world-class
music is free, or you can throw a buck in
the basket. You can stop by office towers
at lunchtime all season and hear musical
groups put on by Trumps and suchlike to
entertain the peons working there. For a
couple of bucks, you can have a coffee
in Paley Park, vestpocket hideaway

with food kiosk 50 yards from St. Thomas
Church, three-minutes by foot from the angels
at Rockefeller Center.

III
Angels at Rockefeller Center? Angels.
Blowing trumpets down the evergreen
raised beds leading away from Fifth Avenue to
the skating rink. Old folks twirling there because
they can, young folk falling down
because they can't. And the angel
flying in bronze above it, as it has for all
my lifetime. The music. The smell of hot pretzels,
hot chestnuts, hot dogs.

IV
It's not really an angel, that bronze figure above
the skating rink. It's Prometheus, bringing fire
to mankind.

V
Beautiful, Rock Center. So full of art and
music and shops purveying the best
man can do. Once, there was Corne de la Toison
d'Or,
the best chocolate. The Best. But then, it left.
Rumour

had it that a family feud killed the Belgian
chocolatier. I don't know. But...well...it's New York.
Other delights took its place. (Well, not really.)

VI
I interviewed for a job once in Rock Center,
in one of the great, grey buildings
holding court plunk in the middle
of Midtown, making a web of all the world
before there was the Web. The AP was where
I went, the Associated Press. I didn't get it; I was
too green. Now I'm too riddled with the
expensive evidence of abundant aging. (Oh,
well.)
So I freelanced. Which allowed me the
Freedom of the City.
Especially at Christmas.

VII
Cheap tickets, aficionado tickets up at the top,
for *The Nutcracker.* They had to be.
It was early days,
and I was usually broke. Hours and hours
spent inside St. Thomas, drinking in
the Anglican splendors
of a French Gothic building,
quiet but for the rumble
of the No. 7 train far below the stone floors.

Christmas in New York (continued)

Beautiful in its quiet, unworldly splendid
when the choir sang
before an altar decked with festal cloths,
embroidered in gold thread,
topped with gold and silver patens, chalices,
before a reredos of two dozen saints
or more
in grey stone, a counterpoint to the rose window
gentling, but improving, the sharp, pale winter
New York sun
slanting down for a few hours
between the sentinel
office buildings darkening Fifth Avenue
one side at a time. A walk
to the carousel in Central Park,
twirling in the snowflakes
while kids screamed in glee and
mothers paced frantically, as mothers do,
outside the pavilion. A long walk
up the East Side to Balto, bronze statue
of a dog, the sled dog that delivered vaccine
to Nome in the
bad old days. I could sit on it.
Everyone sat on it.
On to the boat lake where kids sailed
radio-controlled
sailboats if the pond had not

iced over yet. A coffee
there.

VIII

New York is coffee. For the price of
coffee, you can watch
the most intricate dances of
humans from inside a cheap cafe,
outdoors at a dear one, or perched
at kiosks dotting the city. Long before Starbucks,
Manhattan did coffee. It's a frantic drink,
but that's not why.
New York is not frantic. It has a heart and soul
of purest calm, the calm of knowing
that no matter what,
it is the center of the universe.
Only those who have tasted the nectar
of desire, and set
off in pursuit,
truly understand.

Other Books by Laura Harrison McBride:

Car Full of Death
A Quirky British Mystery Romp.
The first in the
Shelf & Chloe Barker Mystery series

Ireland Explained
Beautiful, ethereal, tragic, strong, fun-loving.
This charming journey reveals it all.

Catfirmations
Affirmations for life, inspired by the wisdom of
felines and the Dartmoor landscape

Please visit our web site:

www.muffindogpress.com

Please visit the author's web site:

www.LauraHarrisonMcBride.com

Printed in Great Britain
by Amazon